LOCKED IN A CAGE

WORDS DEFINED THROUGH POETRY

MANNAN MEHTANI

To my family and friends,

Thank you for being a source of strength, encouragement, and support throughout my writing journey. Your unwavering faith in me has been an invaluable asset, and I couldn't have done it without you. This book is dedicated to you with love and gratitude.

Contents

Contents

Contents

Preface

This book is a collection of thoughts and musings that have been lovingly put together to form a unique narrative that will take you on a journey of discovery and self-reflection. Through these poems, I hope to bring to life the beauty of the human experience in a way that is both poetic and meaningful. I invite you to find within these pages something that resonates with your heart and soul and encourages you to explore your own emotions and beliefs. Enjoy the journey!!

1. In Nature's Lap

Nature's beauty so serene
Bringing smiles to hearts unseen
Colours of trees and skies so blue
Giving us sights so grand and true
Breezes blowing through the air
Making us stop and just stare
The chirps of birds so full of glee
Sing to us of sweet harmony
The beauty of the rising sun
Turns the sky a brilliant hue
As the colours start to dance and play
We feel joy and hope today
The rolling hills and lush green grass
Bring us to a place of peace
Where we can find tranquillity
And within ourselves, a place to be
Nature's beauty so divine
Our spirits will forever shine
For in the beauty we behold
We find peace in the stories told.

2. The Scent Of Rain

The scent of rain, like no other
Fills me with joy, my heart is full
The sweet smell of wet grass, a cover
A feeling of calm, a soothing lull
The smell of the air, so clean
The soft pitter-patter on the roof
The sound of the thunder, so serene
The gentle breeze, a light aloof
The smell of the rain, so divine
A refreshing start to a new day
My worries linger, no longer mine
As I take a deep breath, I can't help but sway
The scent of rain, a reminder of love
A reminder of hope in the sky above
A reminder of life, a reminder of peace
A reminder of nature, a reminder of ease.

3. That Sweet Corner Of The House

That sweet corner of the house,
Where I made most of my memories,
A place of solace and comfort,
Where I could be me.
A place of laughter and joy,
Where I could be free,
A place of peace and serenity,
Where I could just be.
A place of dreams and aspirations,
Where I could explore my creativity,
A place of hope and ambition,
Where I could find my destiny.
A place of love and understanding,
Where I could find my true identity,
A place of warmth and security,
Where I could find my inner strength.
That sweet corner of the house,
Where I made most of my memories,
A place of comfort and joy,
Where I could be me.

4. So Grand A Day

A happy tale I'll tell you now
Of a day that was so grand
A day that was so full of joy
It was hard to understand
The sun was shining bright and clear
The birds were singing sweet
The sky was blue and the air was warm
It was a day so complete
The family gathered round the table
To share a meal and a laugh
The children were so full of joy
It was a moment to savour and gaff
The day was filled with laughter and love
And stories that were shared
The family was so close and tight
It was a moment that was so rare
The day was so full of joy
It was hard to comprehend
The family was so happy and content
It was a day that was so grand

5. Natural Elation

The serene blue sky, so vast and wide,
A sight to behold from far and wide.
The sun's rays glisten, a sight so divine,
A sight that's so hard to define.
The ocean, so deep and blue,
A sight that's so grand and true.
The waves crash against the shore,
A sight that's so peaceful and pure.
The birds, so graceful and free,
A sight that's so beautiful to see.
Their wings soar through the air,
A sight that's so rare and fair.
The serene blue sky, the ocean, and the birds,
A sight that's so majestic and unheard.
A sight that's so tranquil and serene,
A sight that's so hard to be seen.

6. Paradise

A paradise of beauty, a place of delight
Where the sun shines bright and the stars shine at night
A place of serenity, a place of peace
Where the birds sing sweetly and the flowers never cease
A paradise of joy, a place of content
Where the rivers flow gently and the mountains are sent
A place of harmony, a place of love
Where the trees sway softly and the sky is above
A paradise of dreams, a place of hope
Where the clouds drift slowly and the wind whispers softly as it
blows
A place of wonder, a place of awe
Where the sunsets are breathtaking and the night sky is in awe
A paradise of life, a place of joy
Where the laughter of children fills the air with joy
A place of beauty, a place of grace
Where the beauty of nature is seen in every place
A paradise of life, a place of dreams
Where the beauty of life is seen in all its gleams
A place of love, a place of peace
Where the beauty of paradise will never cease.

7. A Better Place

The world is a place of beauty and grace,
Where we can all find a place to embrace.
But too often we forget our place,
And the world is left in a state of disgrace.
We must take action to make the world a better place,
Where everyone can find a safe space.
Where we can all come together and share,
And show that we all truly care.
We must strive to create a world of peace,
Where everyone can find release.
Where we can all live in harmony,
And find a way to be free.
We must work together to make the world a better place,
Where everyone can find a place.
Where we can all come together and unite,
And make sure that everyone has the right to fight.
We must take action to make the world a better place,
Where everyone can find a safe space.
Where we can all come together and share,
And show that we all truly care.

8. Manifest

Hey universe, have you ever thought of me?
Or am I just a tiny speck in your grand scheme?
I feel so small, a minuscule part
Amidst your vast galaxies and stars so bright
My life, so insignificant, a mere blink of an eye
In your eternity, am I worth your time?
Sometimes I feel lost and confused,
My worries and anxieties, I'm sure you've seen
But I have a hope, a faith, a prayer
That in your grace, you haven't forgotten me
Hey universe, have you ever thought of me?
I may not be much, but you know, I'm trying to be.

9. Brotherhood

Beauty of brotherhood,
It's a bond that will never be misunderstood.
From the mountains to the sea,
We all must come together in unity,
It's the one thing that will keep us sane,
In this world of chaos and pain.
Brotherhood, it brings us all closer,
It brings us joy and much more,
It's the one thing that will never die,
Until we reach the other side.
It's a bond that's so true,
It helps us get through,
In times of need and despair,
It shows us that we care.
Brotherhood, it will never break,
It will never falter or shake,
It's a bond that's so strong,
It will last forever, so move along.

10. See Me Fall

People who want to see me fall,
Want to lay me down and bury me,
My spirit's strong, I won't give in,
I'll rise up and be free.
I won't be broken, I won't be cowed,
I'll stand tall and proud,
I'll never give in to their taunts,
I'll never be brought down.
They may try to bring me down,
But I'll never be defeated,
My courage will never waver,
My strength will never be depleted.
I'll keep my head held high,
And never give in to despair,
I'll keep my faith and courage,
And never give up hope, no matter what they dare.

11. Worth Nothing

I have no worth, I am nothing,
Empty and void of any meaning,
My value and worth, what do they bring?
My life is wasted, lost at sea,
My worth, I can never agree,
A worthless life, what can I be?
My value, it's gone and I'm left with none,
I'm nothing, I'm not the chosen one,
I'm worth nothing, that can't be undone.
My life is a waste, I'm stuck in a rut,
My worth, it's something that I just can't compute,
No matter how hard I try, I'm still worth naught.
My worth, it's been taken from me,
I'm nothing, I have no dignity,
My life is a waste, my worth can never be seen.
My worth, I cannot define,
I'm nothing, I'm a worthless sign,
My life, it's been taken away, my worth, it has been denied.

12. Getting up

I was down, I was out, I was lost in the crowd
My spirit was broken, my heart was so loud
I felt like I was stuck in a never-ending cloud
But I knew I had to get back on my feet
I had to find the strength to stand up and compete
I had to learn to be strong and never retreat
So I started to build myself up, piece by piece
I worked hard and I never ceased
I was determined to find my own peace
I learned to be resilient and never give in
I learned to be brave and never give up again
I learned to be patient and never give in to sin
And I kept learning, I kept growing
I kept pushing, I kept going
I kept striving, I kept knowing
That I could make it, I could do it
I could be strong, I could be true
I could learn continuo and make it through
And now I'm standing tall, I'm standing proud
I'm standing strong, I'm standing loud
I'm standing firm, I'm standing proud
I'm back on my feet, I'm back in the game

I'm back in the fight, I'm back in the frame
I'm back in the race, I'm back in the lane
And I'm learning continuo, I'm learning to grow
I'm learning to be strong, I'm learning to know
That I can make it, I can do it, I can go

13. The Revolt

A man of innocence, taken advantage of,
His heart and soul, so often scoffed.
He's been pushed and pulled, and taken for granted,
His spirit broken, his will recanted.
He's been taken for granted, his trust betrayed,
His life a cycle of pain and dismay.
He's been taken advantage of, his life a mess,
His heart and soul, a never-ending stress.
He's had enough, he's had his fill,
He's ready to take back his will.
He's ready to turn himself to the ultimate worse,
Ready to take back what's been taken from him first.
He's ready to take back his life,
Ready to take back his strife.
He's ready to take back his power,
Ready to take back his hour.

14. Another Love

My heart is aching, my soul is torn,
For another love I have been born.
My heart is heavy, my mind is weak,
For another love I must seek.
My eyes are searching, my heart is yearning,
For another love I am yearning.
My heart is broken, my soul is lost,
For another love I must pay the cost.
My heart is aching, my soul is in pain,
For another love I must remain.
My heart is heavy, my mind is confused,
For another love I must be used.
My eyes are searching, my heart is aching,
For another love I must be taking.
My heart is broken, my soul is in despair,
For another love I must prepare.
My heart is aching, my soul is in turmoil,
For another love I must toil.
My heart is heavy, my mind is in doubt,
For another love I must go without.

15. If We Fell In Love

If we fell in love,
It would be like a dove,
Soaring through the sky,
Our hearts would never die.
We'd be like two stars,
Twinkling in the night,
Our love would be so bright,
It would be a beautiful sight.
We'd be like two birds,
Chirping in the trees,
Our love would be so sweet,
It would bring us to our knees.
We'd be like two flowers,
Blooming in the sun,
Our love would be so strong,
It would never be undone.
We'd be like two waves,
Crashing on the shore,
Our love would be so deep,
It would last forevermore.

16. Poetry In Those Eyes

It is time that I need with you
I can only give time and time is what I don't have...
I try to get away
But you manage to pull me back
I see poetry in those eyes
And all that beautiful madness
Tangled in your deep black hair
You lie to me with those catlike eyes
And I still believe whatever you say
Tried ignoring you but ,
Whenever my mind wandered ,
It always found its way back to you.
I think about you everyday
I plan out what to say
You have no idea what I go through
I try not to stare, I try not to hide
I try not to look at your gram wall everyday
I wish I had told you earlier
Perhaps we might not have been the same today.

17. My Priorities Are Set

My priorities are set,
I'm not here to play your game,
I'm not here to be your pet,
I'm not here to take the blame.
I'm here to do what's best for me,
To make sure I'm living life right,
I'm here to make sure I'm free,
To make sure I'm living life bright.
I'm not here to be your toy,
I'm not here to be your fool,
I'm not here to be your ploy,
I'm not here to be your tool.
I'm here to make sure I'm strong,
To make sure I'm living life right,
I'm here to make sure I'm long,
To make sure I'm living life bright.
I'm not here to be your friend,
I'm not here to be your date,
I'm not here to be your end,
I'm not here to be your mate.
I've my priorities set,
I don't have time for you,

MANNAN MEHTANI

I'm here to make sure I'm set,
To make sure I'm living life true.

18. Just Friends

We were just friends, no more, no less
A bond that was strong, yet so hard to express
We shared secrets, laughs, and tears
But never could we admit our fears
We were just friends, no more, no less
A friendship that was so hard to confess
We talked for hours, but never said goodbye
We were so close, yet so far apart, why?
We were just friends, no more, no less
A relationship that was so hard to address
We shared stories, but never our hearts
We were so close, yet so far apart
We were just friends, no more, no less
A bond that was so hard to express
We shared moments, but never our souls
We were so close, yet so far apart, why?
We were just friends, no more, no less
A friendship that was so hard to confess
We shared memories, but never our dreams
We were so close, yet so far apart, why?
We were just friends, no more, no less
A relationship that was so hard to address

We shared laughter, but never our love
We were so close, yet so far apart, why?

• 21 •

19. One Sided Love

My heart is aching, my soul is sore
For I am in love, but love is no more
My love is unrequited, my feelings ignored
My heart is broken, my dreams are floored
I gave my all, but it was not enough
My love was one-sided, I was out of touch
My heart was open, my feelings were true
But my love was not returned, what else could I do?
I tried to move on, but I could not forget
The love I had for you, I could not regret
My heart was broken, my dreams were crushed
My love was one-sided, I was left in the dust
I want to hold your hand and never let go,
But I know that will never happen, oh no.
My love for you is strong and true,
But all of it is just for me, not for you.
I thought I could move on, but I was wrong
My love for you was still strong
My heart was heavy, my soul was sore
For I was in love, but love was no more
My heart aches with a deep despair,
Knowing that I will never have you near.

But I keep my love for you alive,
Knowing that one day it will survive.

20. Three Questions

Three questions to her, I must ask
To understand the truth of our past
The first one, what did we mean to each other?
Was it love, or just a passing weather?
The second one, why did we part?
Was it something I said, or something you heard?
The third one, what do you think of me now?
Do you still care, or have you forgotten how?
The answers I seek, I may never find
But I'll keep searching, until the end of time
For the truth of our past, I must know
So I can move on, and let go.

21. Betrayal

Betrayal is a cruel thing,
It takes away a part of you,
It leaves you feeling so alone,
And wondering what to do.
It's a feeling of total despair,
And a deep sense of deceit,
It's a wound that doesn't heal,
And leaves your heart incomplete.
It's a feeling of utter shock,
As if you've been hit by a truck,
It's a pain that never goes away,
No matter how hard you try to duck.
Betrayal, a word that's so cold,
A word that can make us feel old.
It's a feeling of loneliness and sadness,
A feeling of complete madness.
It's a feeling of being betrayed,
Of having your trust taken away,
It's a wound that never really heals,
And leaves you feeling so betrayed.
But even in the face of betrayal,
There is still hope in the end,

For through forgiveness and understanding,
The wounds can start to mend.

22. The Breakup

I thought we had a connection,
A bond that could not be broken,
But you left me in the dark,
Without a single word or spark.
I thought we had a future,
A path that we could explore,
But you left me in the dust,
Without a single thought or trust.
I thought we had a chance,
A chance to make it right,
But you left me in the cold,
Without a single touch or hold.
I thought we had a love,
A love that could never die,
But you left me in the void,
Without a single goodbye.
I thought we had a bond,
A bond that could never be broken,
But you left me in the shadows,
Without a single word or token.

23. Stressed Out

Stressed out, I feel my world start to spin,
My mind so full of worries, I can't seem to win.
My body aching, my head pounding,
The pressure and the fear, my heart pounding.
My head is spinning, I'm so confused
My body's shaking, I'm so abused
My stomach's churning, I'm so scared
I'm feeling so lost, no one has cared
The days just seem to drag on,
The nights, long and empty, I am so gone.
Tired and worn, I just want to sleep,
But the burden of stress keeps me awake and weep.
My chest is tight, I'm so alone
My breathing is shallow, I'm on my own
My eyes are heavy, I'm so tired
I'm feeling so helpless, I'm so wired
I try to focus on the good,
But the bad keeps taking me back to the hood.
My thoughts in a fog, my mood so low,
My body can't take this anymore, I just want to go.
Stressed out, is an understatement,
It seems like this feeling will never abate.

But I will keep fighting, no matter the cost,
For I know that I can make it, no matter the loss.

24. My Dark Phase

My dark phase
A time that I wish I could erase
It's a road that I'm still trying to find my way
It's been a difficult journey, and I still don't know what to say.
A heavy fog that I can't seem to shake
My emotions are a tangled mess, and I'm broken beyond repair
The days seem to blend together, and I can't find the air.
My thoughts are chaotic and my outlook so bleak
I try to keep my chin up, but it's hard to be meek
I feel scared and alone, with no one to turn to
The darkness has taken hold, and I don't know what to do
But I will continue on, and find a way out
I will fight through this darkness and find light, without a doubt
I won't let my dark phase be the only thing I'm known for
I'll rise above and come out of this, I'm sure.

25. A Life In Isolation

Alone in my room, I sit in my chair
The walls are my only companion, no one else is there
The silence is deafening, I can't hear a sound
My thoughts are my only company, they swirl around
The days pass by, one after the other
My loneliness is a heavy burden, like a boulder
I try to keep busy, but nothing can fill the void
My heart is heavy, my spirit is destroyed
Oftentimes I'd pause and wonder,
Why I'm gone and not with others.
My days filled with pain and hunger,
Only my thoughts as my bother.
The world seemed so far away,
I'd dream of being among them.
But I remained confined in my own way,
Leaning on hope to see the end.
The sun shined and the moon glowed,
My only solace was in nature.
The birds would sing and the wind would blow,
A reminder of life's fragile beauty.
Isolation has shaped me in many ways,
A unique experience that I must face.

Though I am still filled with fear and dismay,
I remain hopeful for a brighter place.

26. If My Wounds Could Talk

If my wounds could talk,
They'd tell a story of pain and strife,
Of a heart that's been broken,
And a soul that's been cut like a knife.
They'd tell of a life that's been hard,
Of a spirit that's been tested and tried,
Of a heart that's been shattered,
And a soul that's been denied.
They'd tell of a love that's been lost,
Of a dream that's been forgotten and gone,
Of a heart that's been broken,
And a soul that's been withdrawn.
If my wounds could talk,
They'd tell a story of pain and sorrow,
Of a heart that's been broken,
And a soul that's been hollow.

27. Over It

It's time to get over it,
Forget the pain and the hurt.
Stop the tears and the yelling,
And take control of life's jolt.
It's time to move forward,
Away from the sorrow and strife.
Put the hurt and the anger
Deep down in memory of life.
It's time to be happy,
To put away the past.
Live life with a smile
And make memories that last.
It's time to get over it,
Don't let the pain stay on.
Forget the tears and the fighting,
And make a new dawn.

28. A New Hope

A new hope shining bright
The future is taking flight
The darkness of the night
Will soon be out of sight
A new hope beckons us
To rise above the fuss
And make the world a better place
With a smile on our face
A new hope is here
To erase all our fears
To bring us peace and joy
Like a brand new toy
A new hope to inspire
To show us what we can aspire
It reminds us we're all connected
And that we're never rejected
A new hope for us all
To take a stand and stand tall
Spread kindness and good cheer
And make the world so much more clear.

29. Those days

Those days were filled with laughter,
The days that we had together,
The days when we were together,
The days we had forever.
We used to walk around the town,
Our laughter could be heard all around,
The days that we never wanted to end,
The days we shared as our friends.
Those days were so special to me,
The days that we spent so carefree,
The days that had no worries,
The days of our sweet memories.
Those days of joy and delight,
The days that gave us such delight,
The days that gave us so much joy,
The days that we will never destroy.
Those days have come and gone,
But those are the days that live on,
The days that we will never forget,
The days that will stay in our hearts forever.

30. What Is Success?

Success is a journey
A tale of dedication
Where obstacles are overcome
And goals are realized with elation
The road to success is not easy
It takes dedication and strength
With hard work and perseverance
You can achieve anything at length
Achieving success is not a single step
It's a long and winding road
With each challenge, we grow
To reach our goals, we must be bold
We must stay focused and strive
To make our dreams come true
No matter what obstacles come our way
We can make it through
Success is a story of courage
When we face our fears
We must have faith in ourselves
And keep pushing through the tears
Success is an anecdote of triumph
A testament to our resolve

We must never give up on our dreams
And never lose sight of our goals

31. Hey Universe!?

Hey universe,
A vast expanse of wonder and mystery,
Full of secrets and beauty,
Beyond our comprehension.
We stand in awe and admiration,
Of your grandeur and majesty,
We feel small and insignificant,
Yet our curiosity is boundless.
We are in awe of your beauty,
The stars, the galaxies and nebulae,
We are mesmerized by your scale,
The sheer enormity of the universe.
We gaze up in wonder,
At the mysteries you hide,
We may never know your secrets,
But we still seek to explore,
For the universe is a playground,
Of marvels and discovery,
We can never truly fathom your depths,
But we are still in awe of your magnificence.
Hey universe,
You are a source of inspiration and beauty,

We will forever be in awe of you,
And your grandeur and mystery.

32. Nervous Wreck

I'm a prisoner of my own thoughts and feelings,
Trapped in a prison of my own making.
My mind is a labyrinth of emotions,
Where I'm forever searching and seeking.
My heart is a caged bird,
Fluttering and beating against the bars.
My soul is a prisoner of my own mind,
Trapped in a prison without stars.
My thoughts are a raging storm,
Tearing through my mind like a hurricane.
My feelings are a raging sea,
Tossing and turning in a never-ending wave.
My mind is a prison of my own making,
Where I'm forever locked in chains.
My heart is a caged bird,
Fluttering and beating against the bars.
My soul is a prisoner of my own thoughts and feelings,
Trapped in a prison without stars.
I'm a prisoner of my own thoughts and feelings,
Forever searching and seeking in vain.

33. Bars

A caged bird, a caged heart,
A caged soul, a caged mind,
A caged teenager, so confined.
The walls are high, the bars are strong,
The feelings of a youth so wrong.
The world outside, so far away,
The feelings of a teen, so astray.
The anger, the fear, the sadness, the pain,
The feelings of a teen, so hard to explain.
The loneliness, the hurt, the shame,
The feelings of a teen, so hard to tame.
The joy, the hope, the love, the dreams,
The feelings of a teen, so hard to redeem.
The courage, the strength, the faith, the will,
The feelings of a teen, so hard to fulfil.
The caged bird, the caged heart,
The caged soul, the caged mind,
The caged teenager, so confined.

34. A Vicious Dreamworld

Living life in a dreamworld,
Where reality is a blur,
Where the lines between truth and lies,
Are often hard to discern.
Where the days are filled with fantasy,
And the nights are filled with dread,
Where the future is uncertain,
And the past is long since dead.
Where the sun never sets,
And the stars never rise,
Where the days are filled with joy,
But the nights are filled with cries.
Where the dreams are never ending,
And the nightmares never cease,
Where the days are filled with laughter,
But the nights are filled with tears.
Where the days are filled with hope,
But the nights are filled with fear,
Where the future is uncertain,
And the past is never clear.

Where the days are filled with beauty,
But the nights are filled with pain,
Where the dreams are never ending,
But the nightmares never wane.
Living life in a dreamworld,
Where reality is a blur,
Where the lines between truth and lies,
Are often hard to discern.

35. Inner Demons and Devils

My inner demons and devils,
They come on days that are not so merry.
They scream in my head and shake my soul,
And make me feel like I'm in a dark, deep hole.
My inner demons and devils,
They try to break me, but I won't let them win.
I'll fight, I'll push, I'll keep going,
And I will not let them take me in.
My inner demons and devils,
Their lies are like spears that pierce my heart.
But I'll be brave, I'll stand my ground,
And I will not let them tear me apart.
My inner demons and devils,
They try to keep me down, but I will rise.
I will be strong and I will be brave,
And I will face them with no fear in my eyes.

36. The Godfather

Oh, The Godfather, so powerful and wise,
He taught us lessons few can realize.
A master of his craft, he left his mark,
His legacy will remain in the dark.
The Don of the Corleones, a leader of men,
His family was his pride, he kept them safe and then.
His willingness to protect and keep his kin,
Was unmatched by anyone, and will never end.
The Godfather was a man of honour and respect,
His moral code was firm and never did he neglect.
His decisions were respected, his word was law,
His actions made the world take pause and awe.
His courage and strength will forever stand,
His principles were strong and remain in the land.
The Godfather will be remembered for generations,
His name will be spoken with admiration.

37. Locked In A Cage

Locked in a cage, so small and tight
I can't find the way out of this plight
I struggle, but nothing can I do
My captor's cruel, his intentions are so cruel
The walls of my prison are cold and bare,
My cries for help, no one seems to care.
I'm stuck in this cage, with no way out,
My life is a prison, I'm filled with doubt.
My wings are clipped and I can't fly
My heart is heavy, my eyes they cry
My wings were made to soar up high
But here I am, stuck in this cage, why?
My heart and spirit are so strong
But I'm powerless, nothing can I do
My life is so hard, my future so bleak
I'm a prisoner, locked in a cage
My spirit is broken, my will is in chains,
My life is a prison, I'm filled with disdain.
My dreams are shattered, my hopes are gone,
My future is bleak, I'm all alone.
Time is ticking, days pass by
I can't escape, I can't even try

LOCKED IN A CAGE

I'm so desperate, I cry out in pain
I'm a prisoner, locked in a cage.

38. Nights Like These

Nights like these, so starry and grand,
When the moon is so bright it lights up the land
The air is so still, the night so serene,
We savour the moment, for it's so divine.
The world is so peaceful, the air so crisp,
No sound can be heard but the gentle night's bliss.
The stars twinkle above, so bright and divine,
We savour the moment, for it's so sublime.
The night is so tranquil, the wind is so light,
We pause in the moment, to take in the sight.
The moon beams above, the sky so clear,
We savour the moment, for it's so sincere.
The night is so magical, so filled with delight,
We marvel at nature and all its might.
The stars glimmer above, so tranquil and bright,
We savour the moment, for it's so divine tonight.

39. Paralysed

Paralysed, my heart did freeze,
Every breath I took, a gentle breeze.
It felt like all the life had gone,
My mind and body, all forlorn.
Aware of it, yet not in control,
My movements frozen, my spirit made whole.
Stuck in a state of total despair,
My emotions lay dormant, neither here nor there.
My heart is broken, my soul is in despair
I'm paralysed thinking about you there
My feelings are tangled, my thoughts are a blur
I'm stuck in a trance, I can't find a cure
My heart is aching, my spirit is weak
I'm paralysed thinking about you deep
My feelings are tangled, my thoughts are a haze
I'm stuck in a loop, I'm in a daze
But I found courage to rise above,
To allow my heart to start to love.
And I faced my fears and embraced the light,
Finally free from the days of night.

40. Homicide

A life cut short, a family left broken
A senseless act, a heart so token
The pain of loss, the grief so real
No words can ease, no way to heal
The tragedy of homicide, no easy way to cope
The shock of violence, the aftermath of hope
The finality of death, so hard to take
A life that's gone, a heart that aches
A killer on the loose, a life so taken
A family left in shock, a life so forsaken
A crime so cruel, a life so gone
A family left in despair, a life so withdrawn
A justice to be served, a life so wronged
A family left in anguish, a life so prolonged
A crime so unjust, a life so ended
A family left in sorrow, a life so mended
The hurt and sorrow, the questions why
The tears that fall, the anguished cry
The emptiness of loss, the pain that burns
The justice that's sought, the killer's turn
So much sadness, so much grief
Too many questions, too few relief

The pain of homicide, a sorrow so deep
A life cut short, a family left to weep.

41. ADHD

ADHD, a disorder that's so hard to see
The struggles it brings, so hard to believe
The suffering and chaos, it can bring each day
The emotional pain, that can never go away
Trying to focus, on the tasks at hand
The mind is so scattered, throughout the land
The inability to concentrate, and the constant need to move
The sufferer feeling like, they're in a vacuum
But the ADHD mind, is so much more
The creative thinking, can open new doors
The unique perspective, that it can bring
Can help the sufferer, become anything
So remember, ADHD is not a curse
It's something that's special, and a bit diverse
Now with understanding, and a bit of care
We can help those with ADHD, live with pride and flair.

42. Paranoia

Paranoia, a dark and twisted thing
It lurks in shadows, a silent sting
It creeps in slowly, a silent foe
It's a fear of the unknown, a feeling of woe
Paranoia increasing, anxiety burning
Heart racing and blood pumping
Flooding the brain with fear and distress
Unable to shake the feeling of unease
Stress and panic, irrational thoughts
The mind spinning with uncertainty and doubt
Overwhelming and consuming, a feeling of dread
Fear of the unknown, unable to proceed
Obsessive thinking, mind in a haze
A never ending cycle of thoughts in a maze
No matter what, unable to escape
A feeling of being constantly under attack
The mind and body, a whirlwind of distress
Feeling helpless and stuck in a mess
Paranoia takes ahold, no way to break free
An emotional prison, no one to set me free.

43. My School Life

A school life full of laughter,
A place of joy and fun,
But underneath the surface,
A darker side begun.
The bullies, they were lurking,
Ready to pounce and strike,
Their words were sharp and cutting,
And their actions weren't so nice.
But the student, he was strong,
His mind was sharp and keen,
He knew that he could rise above,
And not be so mean.
He worked hard and studied,
And he never gave up,
He faced the bullies head on,
And he never gave in.
He grew in strength and courage,
And his confidence grew too,
He became the strongest minded student,
And he knew what to do.
He faced the bullies with grace,
And he never backed down,

He showed them that he was strong,
And that he wouldn't be pushed around.
The student had come so far,
From a school life full of laughter,
To becoming the strongest minded student,
And he had done it ever after.

44. A Day In The Life Of A Protagonist

A day in the life of a protagonist
A typical day starts with a cup of coffee,
A brief review of the news to see.
The day ahead is full of mystery,
A potential conflict waiting to be.
The protagonist sets out to complete the task,
A journey of courage and a risk to bask.
He faces his fears and takes the plunge,
A hero's journey with a humble grumble.
The quest continues as he moves on,
Making new allies and foes along.
He perseveres to reach his goal,
A test of strength and a test of soul.
The sun sets and the day is done,
The protagonist is victorious, he has won.
He has achieved his aim and the mission is complete,
A day in the life of a protagonist, a feat.

45. A World Of Misery

A world of misery, so dark and dreary,
Where sorrow and pain are the only things seen.
Where the sun never shines, and the sky is always grey,
Where hope is lost and dreams are never seen.
A world of misery, a place of pain,
Where sorrow reigns, and all is in vain.
The bleakness looms, a deep despair,
A sadness that's felt everywhere.
The wind howls through a broken sky,
A reminder of our misery.
The sun sets, and darkness creeps,
The terror of our future weeps.
The broken dreams and shattered lives,
The pain we can't outrun, it survives.
The weight of the world upon our backs,
A burden that we can't attack.
A world of misery, a place of woe,
Where nothing feels like it should go.
Our hope fades, and hearts break,
In a world where all is at stake.

46. The Hard Truth

The hard truth is sometimes hard to face,

It can leave us feeling so out of place.

It's a bitter pill that we must swallow,

No matter how hard it may be to follow.

No matter how much we wish it away,

The truth is still there, here to stay.

It can be hard to accept our mistakes,

And to learn from them, we must take.

The truth can hurt, yes that is true,

But it can also help us to break through.

It can be a scary and daunting thing,

But it can also set us free and give us wings.

So when the hard truth comes to call,

We must accept it, no matter how tall.

It may take time, but it's worth the wait,

For the truth can be an invaluable weight.

47. Red Pill

A choice of two, a red and blue,
A path of life, what will you choose?
The red pill, a path of truth,
A journey of discovery, what will you do?
A world of secrets, hidden away,
A world of lies, what will you say?
The red pill, a path of knowledge,
A journey of understanding, what will you see?
A world of pain, a world of strife,
A world of darkness, what will you find?
The red pill, a path of courage,
A journey of strength, what will you do?
A world of truth, a world of light,
A world of freedom, what will you fight?
The red pill, a path of power,
A journey of courage, what will you choose?

48. The Matrix

A world of technology,
a world of code The Matrix, the place of digital mode
Where the rules of reality no longer apply
And the secrets of life can be deciphered with a try
A world of virtual dreams, a world of fantasy
Where the fate of mankind lies in the hands of a few
A world of powerful computers and artificial intelligence
Where the decisions of life can be made without a defence
A world of infinite possibilities and dreams of greatness
Where a person can be who they want and live as they wish
A world of knowledge and power, a world of mystery
Where the truth of life can be unearthed, if you have the key
A world of deception, a world of deceit
Where the truth is hidden, and the lies are complete
A place of shadows, a place of fear
Where the truth is hidden, and the lies are clear
A world where the lines between reality and fiction blur
Where the boundaries of life can be pushed and explored
A world of choices, a world of freedom
Where the power of The Matrix can be felt in every season.

49. Being The Eldest Son

Eldest son I am, of a large family,
Though I have much more responsibility,
It's a great honour, and I carry it with pride,
I'll never let emotion be my guide.
The eldest son is the one who stands out
Carrying the weight of their family's clout
The one who sets the example, the one who sets the trend
The one who's expected to make the right moves in the end.
My siblings look up to me, for I'm their guide,
I am the one who must always decide,
I'm the leader in this family of mine,
And I'll do my best to make it all shine.
I take my role very seriously,
For I'm the eldest son, I'm expected to be,
My parents depend on me, they can trust,
That I'll be the one that they can trust.
I'm the role model, and I take that to heart,
Always doing my best to stay on the right path,
My siblings look to me for advice and direction,
So I'm sure to show them the right connection.
Being the eldest son, is a great responsibility,
And I'm proud to carry it with sincerity,

It's a role I take seriously, and I'm proud,
For I'm the eldest son, and I'll wear it loud.

50. A Good Life

This is the way to have a good life,
To spread love, peace, and joy,
That's why brotherhood is the key,
It's the way to a life of glee.
Be kind and generous to all,
And be a shining beacon of hope,
Let the world be your oyster,
And never let fear of failure be a cope.
Always strive for something greater,
Be it success, or just a smile,
Take a step back and feel the moments,
Just take a break after a while.
Be open to new experiences,
And learn from your mistakes,
Sometimes you may stumble and fall,
But that's the beauty of a life well made.
Live it to the fullest,
For the time is now and fleeting,
Make every second count,
And you'll have a life worth keeping.

51. The Unlucky Bandit

The unlucky bandit in the night
Never saw the light of day
He sought his fortune, but it never came
His luck had gone astray
He tried his luck in the old west
Where lawmen were tough and mean
But no matter how hard he tried
His luck was never seen
He roamed the hills and the plains
In search of a way to get by
But no matter how hard he tried
His luck was always gone dry
The unlucky bandit was always on the run
But his luck had never changed
No matter how hard he tried
His luck was always the same
Though the unlucky bandit's luck never came
His spirit was strong and true
And he taught us a lesson we'll never forget
That luck is never due.

52. Utopia

The world is a perfect place,
A utopia without a trace
Of fear or hate or doubt,
Where joy and peace reigns throughout.
Where love is the only law,
And inequality no more
Where everyone is treated fair,
Where kindness is always there.
Where laughter, smiles and hugs,
Outweighs the sadness and rugs
Where every voice is heard,
Where every dream is stirred.
Where everyone can be free,
And their uniqueness can be seen
Where no one is judged,
Where acceptance is just.
Where respect is given,
Equality in all is driven
A world where we can thrive,
And peace is the only strive.

53. Nightmares

Nightmares haunt my dreams,
Like a dark, sinister theme.
They come when I'm sleeping,
My mind begins to weep.
Lurking in the shadows,
My fear starts to grow.
The terror and dread,
I can't seem to let go.
I toss and turn in bed,
My heart is racing fast.
I try to scream,
But no sound comes past.
The nightmares fill my head,
Like an evil force.
I can't seem to break free,
It's like I'm under its spell.
The darkness and despair,
I'm forever in its grasp.
It sucks away my hope,
And leaves me in its wake.
But I still have faith,
That this nightmare will pass.

And I'll wake up in the morning,
The terror and fear will be gone at last.

• 68 •

54. Rags to riches

Rags to riches, a dream within reach
A story of success, of hardships beneath
From poverty to opulence, a journey of goals
A chance to prove that you have control
It takes strength and courage, determination and luck
To rise from the bottom and reach the top of the buck
It's a long and winding road, you'll face many a test
But never forget, you're the one that knows best
You must stay true to yourself, and never give in
Keep your head up high, and don't let them win
All of your hard work will pay off in the end
For your story of rags to riches, no one can contend
It's not easy, it's not quick, but the reward is immense
Push through the struggle, and you'll reach your defence
Your dreams will be realized, and your story will inspire
For your rags to riches tale, you'll never retire.

55. Run For The Money

Run for the money, run for the gold,
The prize at the end, so worth the toll.
It's a race that none can afford to ignore,
The finish line just a little bit more.
The competition is fierce and the stakes are high,
Your heart beating fast, no room for a sigh.
Run for the money, run for the thrill,
Soon you will see, you have the skill.
Your future's at stake and you must win,
The money you need, you mustn't give in.
Run for the money, you can do it,
Put your all in and you'll make it through it.
The finish line is just ahead,
Your victory's close, you'll soon be led.
Run for the money, run for the win,
Your hard work will pay off, it's worth it in the end.

56. Knock of the devil

Knock of the devil, sounding so strong,
For every person, it's a different song.
It tries to lure you in, to it's dark embrace,
It's seductive whispers, a cruel race.
You feel it in your soul, your heart, your mind,
The devil's call, it's so hard to find.
It's siren song, so tempting, so sweet,
It's a dark and lonely path, no one to meet.
It's a path of destruction, of chaos and pain,
The devil's call, it will remain.
It will whisper of power, of wealth and fame,
But in the end, it's all a game.
Don't be fooled by the devil's lies,
It will only lead to tears and cries.
Listen to the angels, they will guide you right,
And keep you away from the devil's blight.

57. Endeavours

I strive to reach the peak of success
To be the best I must pass the test
I'm highly ambitious and I will not rest
Until I see the fruits of my quest
My goals seem daunting, I'm scared to fail
But I know I will prevail
My ambition will never fail
Pushing me forward, I will not trail
My determination is strong, I will fight
Through any challenge, no matter how slight
My ambition is my might
Leading me to the height
I will cross every hurdle, no matter the size
My ambition will be my guide
My aim is to win, never to hide
No matter the difficulty, I will not abide
I will stay focused, never give in
My ambition will keep me in the win
My dreams will come true, I will see
My ambition will always be the key.

58. Perspectives

Perspectives are a funny thing,
Everyone has their own to bring.
It shapes how we see the world,
And the joys and chaos that we swirl.
We can look at any situation,
And come up with a unique interpretation.
It can be as different as night and day,
And can show us a new way.
Perceptions are not always right,
But they can help us in our plight.
If we look at things in a different light,
We can see solutions, clear and bright.
No one perspective is correct,
But the truth can be found in a complex.
When we have all the pieces of the puzzle,
We can see a much larger picture.

59. Love Holds No

Love holds no boundaries,
No walls, no fences, no gates.
It transcends all boundaries,
Of race, of class, of age.
Love holds no limits,
No divides, no barriers, no stops.
It knows no bounds,
From end to end, from top to bottom.
Love holds no grudges,
No resentment, no ill will.
It brings no judgement,
No measure, no comparison to fill.
Love holds no labels,
No titles, no names, no brand.
It speaks its own language,
A whisper, a touch, an understanding hand.
Love holds no rules,
No expectations, no conditions to meet.
It is an unconditional offering,
A never-ending, beautiful, unique treat.

60. League of Legends

I come to join the League of Legends today
A place where champions fight in their own way
Where battles are fought in the Summoner's Rift
Where the fierce battle of mind and strength begins
A place of tactics, strategy and skill
The greatest warriors come to test their will
A platform to showcase their mastery
Where the victor is the one with destiny
The league is full of champions of all kinds
From mages to marksmen and tanks they bring
Each one with their own strength and skill
Each one ready to take their own kill
The clash of champions is a sight to behold
Where the strongest reign and the weakest fold
Where the battle for victory is never done
And the League of Legends is never won

61. Greed

Greed is a lust that can never be filled
It will take and take and take until there's nothing left to kill
It's a relentless force that can never be quenched
It will always be here, no matter how much we try to prevent
It will make you do things that you never thought you'd do
It will often lead to the worst, even if you don't have a clue
It will never be satisfied, no matter how much you get
It will always want more and more, it will never forget
Greed never stops and it never rests
It will always be around, no matter how hard you try to suppress
You can never truly get rid of it, no matter what you try
It will always be around, it will never die.

62. The Wrath Of God

The Lord of Hosts is just and fair,
His wrath can shake the very air.
When He unleashes His anger,
It can strike with mighty danger.
His power is always on display,
As His wrath can make the heavens sway.
The Lord is not one to forgive,
For His wrath is a fearful thing to live.
The Lord will bring about justice and peace,
But if you don't repent, your soul won't cease.
His wrath is fierce and it will sear,
So don't defy Him, and show Him fear.
The Lord will show no mercy and be severe,
For His wrath will bring your soul to fear.
His awesome might will be seen,
As He unleashes His wrath and His vengeance.

63. Pull The Trigger

Pull the trigger, a sign of despair
A weapon of destruction, never to repair
The trigger's been pulled, a life taken away
A family destroyed, with no words to say
The trigger's been pulled, a ripple of shock
Hearts heavy with sorrow, a nightmare to mock
The trigger so easily, in a single breathe
The world will never be the same, it won't ever be
Pull the trigger, a decision of death
An end to a life, a final breath
The trigger's been pulled, no more to come
A life forever lost, in an instance gone
Pull the trigger, the only way out
A desperate decision, no doubt about
The trigger's been pulled, a life put to rest
A heavy heart, one last request.

64. Treachery

A snake in the grass, a vile creature
Stabbing in the back, what a feature
A malicious soul, a conniving mind
An untrustworthy self, one of a kind
A heart of stone, a face of deceit
A hidden blade, so sharp and discrete
A silent assassin, no one hears his plea
A cowardly act, a life of treachery
Weaving webs of lies, deceiving those around
A master manipulator, no one makes a sound
A wolf in sheep's clothing, a mask to hide
A pact of deceit, no one to confide
A dark and twisted path, one of foul play
A wicked game, betrayal does not pay
Though justice will prevail, in the end
For those who practice treachery, no reprieve to send.

65. Regardless

Regardless of what others may say
We have to remain true to our own way
We have to stay strong in our beliefs
Regardless of the way others perceive
Regardless of what the future may bring
We must stand firm and remain strong
For our path is for us to decide
Regardless of the advice of others outside
Regardless of what life may bring
We have to have faith and just keep going
For our lives are ours to create
Regardless of the choices that others may make
Regardless of how hard it may get
We have to keep our courage and not forget
That our lives are ours to live
Regardless of what anyone else may give.

66. Devil's Work

Devil's work is done in the dark,
His schemes are often quite stark.
He'll take away your joy and peace,
So watch out — do not be deceived.
His lies and twisted words will try,
To lead you to a place you'll die.
He'll make you think it's in your best,
But it's a wicked, devious test.
He'll whisper in your ear and try,
To make you doubt and wonder why.
He'll fill you with fear and shame,
And your heart will be in flames.
But don't buy into his evil plan,
For it's not worth it in the end.
His work is done in the dark,
But remember to stay strong and be true to your heart.

67. Decisions Of Torment

Decisions of torment, make me so weary

My mind in a storm, never so dreary

I'm stuck between two, both so confusing

One is in front of me, one I'm refusing

My heart is in pain, my soul in strife

My dreams and my goals, my future's life

I'm tempted to go, I'm pushed to stay

Is this a choice that I can make

I'm torn in two, I don't know what to do

I'm in the dark, I can't see the truth

My gut says stay, my heart says leave

My brain says nothing, I'm in disbelief I

'm running out of time, I'm out of patience

I must make a decision, I'm filled with frustration

I'm so scared of the consequences

What will be the outcome, the result of my decisions

68. Labyrinth

Lost in the labyrinth I explore
A journey of winding pathways galore
Twisting and turning, I can't find the light
The pathway so dark, I can't find the sight
The path ahead so murky and bleak
With no indication of where I should seek
A way out of this dark, mysterious maze
A way to the truth, I must appraise
The walls so tall, the path so narrow
I feel so small, and so I holler
The echo of my voice, reverberates through the hall
But nothing comes back, not even a call
The walls around me, I can't break through
This maze is so vast, I can't even view
A way out of here, I'm desperate to find
But I'm so lost, I can't even unwind
But I'll keep searching, my journey will last
Until I find the way out of this vast
Labyrinth and make my way back to the light
Where hopefully I can survive this night.

69. Vendetta

Vengeance, my sweet revenge
It's what I crave night and day
My heart will never rest
Until I have it, my way
I'll take it slow and steady
I'll make you hurt and cry
I'll take all you have
And you won't even know why
I'll make you pay for your wrongs
And watch your world fall apart
I'll take you down with me
And I won't show you any heart
Vengeance, my sweet revenge
It's what I live for each day
My heart will never rest
Until I have it, my way.

70. Final Thoughts

My final thoughts are a swirl of emotion,
A cacophony of memories and devotion.
The past is a blur, a distant dream,
The future a mystery, a distant gleam.
The present is a moment of clarity,
A chance to reflect on what I see.
The choices I've made, the paths I've taken,
The lessons I've learned, the bridges I've broken.
The joys and the sorrows, the highs and the lows,
The moments of triumph, the moments of woe.
The people I've met, the places I've been,
The love I've shared, the pain I've seen.
My final thoughts are a bittersweet blend,
A reflection of life, a journey to the end.
The memories I've made, the moments I've shared,
The love I've given, the lessons I've dared.
My final thoughts are a reminder of life,
A reminder of love, a reminder of strife.
The moments of joy, the moments of pain,
The moments of sorrow, the moments of gain.
My final thoughts are a reminder of me,
A reminder of all that I can be.

The choices I make, the paths I take,
The moments I share, the memories I make

My sincerest thanks for taking the time to explore the depths of this book. I hope that you enjoyed it and found it to be a worthwhile experience. With warmest regards,

Sincerely,

Mannan Mehtani